EMOTIONAL TRAUMA:

Master your emotions to overcome emotional trauma

Debbie John

Table of content

Chapter 1
Chapter 2
Chapter 3

Chapter 1
What is traumatic pressure?

Traumatic pressure is an ordinary response to a strange occasion. Normally, side effects get better with time, however, individuals with additional serious side effects might require proficient assistance. Throughout a lifetime, it's generally expected as be presented to a horrible mishap, whether it is a fierce demonstration, a serious physical issue, a sexual infringement, or other stunning occasions. Accordingly, many will encounter horrible pressure an ordinary response to a strange occasion.

Individuals might try and experience horrible pressure simply by seeing a profoundly upsetting occasion or having a nearby relative or companion experience such an occasion.

In the long stretches of time following such an injury, it's normal for individuals to have a whirlwind of eccentric feelings and actual side effects. They include:

Sadness Feeling
anxious, nervous, or
on high
alertIrritability or
anger
Difficulty sleeping
Relationship
problems
Intrusive
contemplations,

flashbacks, or
nightmares
Trouble feeling good
emotions Avoiding
individuals, spots,
recollections, or
considerations
related to the awful
mishap
Generally, these side
effects get better

with time. In any case, for certain individuals, more extraordinary side effects wait or obstruct their day-to-day routines and don't disappear all alone. Certain individuals might foster intense

pressure issues in
which they have
outrageous side
effects of pressure
that essentially
obstruct day-to-day
existence, school,
work, or social
working in the
month after a
horrendous mishap.

Others can create
post-traumatic
stress disorder
(PTSD), with side
effects that disrupt
day-to-day existence
and keep going for
over a month after
the injury.

Chapter 2
How to recognize whether you are experiencing traumatic stress

Changes in physical and emotional responses will occur:

- becoming quickly surprised or terrified.
- being on high alert for danger.
- self-destructive habits, such as binge drinking or speeding.
- difficulty sleeping.

- Having trouble focusing.
- irritability, explosive anger, or aggressive conduct.
- overwhelming shame or guilt.

Chapter 3
How to deal with traumatic stress

The good news is
that there are some
of highly successful
coping mechanisms
and trauma-related
stressor treatments
available. These

behaviors, according to psychologists and other studies, can help:

Lean on your family. Choose your family or friends as your source of support. If you're ready, you could share your experience and your sentiments with them regarding the tragic event. To reduce some of your everyday stress, you can also enlist the assistance of loved ones for household chores or other responsibilities.Embrace your emotions.

It's common to desire to forget about a horrible experience. On the other hand, staying inside all day, isolating oneself from family and friends, and abusing drugs to block out reminders are not

long-term coping
mechanisms.
Avoidance is
common, but too
much of it might
make you more
stressed and prevent
you from getting
well. Try to ease
back into your
routine gradually.

As you get back into the swing of things, support from family members or a mental health professional can be quite beneficial. Place self-care first. Try your best to eat wholesome meals, engage in regular exercise, and get a restful night's sleep. Additionally, look into alternative constructive coping mechanisms including art, music, meditation, rest, and outdoor activities. Be tolerant. Keep in

mind that an
upsetting event can
cause you to
respond strongly. As
you heal, take each
day as it comes.
Your symptoms
should begin to
gradually get better
as the days go by.